The Ecstasy of Skeptics

The Ecstasy of Skeptics

POEMS

STEVEN HEIGHTON

For Naomi—

Hope your own poetry
grew well in
2011!—

yours,
[signature]

Anansi

First published in 1994 by
House of Anansi Press Limited
34 Lesmill Road
North York, ON
M3B 2T6
(416) 445-3333

Second printing April 1998

Canadian Cataloguing in Publication Data

Heighton, Steven, 1961–
The ecstasy of skeptics

Poems.
ISBN 0-88784-560-6

I. Title.

PS8565.E45E37 1994   C811'.54   C94-932124-9
PR9199.3.H45E37 1994

Editing: Michael Redhill and Don McKay
Cover concept: Angel Guerra
Cover design: Brant Cowie / ArtPlus Limited
Cover illustration: Don Maynard, Lovers' Embrace

Printed and bound in Canada

*House of Anansi Press gratefully acknowledges the
support of the Canada Council for the Arts and the
Ontario Arts Council for our publishing program.*

for my parents

and in memory of Tom Marshall
(1938-1993)

Contents

The Ecstasy of Skeptics

OPENINGS

How shall we sing?

—— Psalm 137

Long Distance Every Sign

Long distance every sign ——
another poem the road gave you.
Another song the aerial
sucked out of sound waves into the car
far gone
on the freeway filed to sand behind your tires
or the forest trail growing in behind you
or the paddles' footprints, fading
in a bay at dawn, as ice knits closed after your stern
and keeps pace ——

At the wheel could you feel above you
the sun's wheel turn
and shuttle you into dark, and home —— and see
the dashboard's green galaxies at dusk
evolving, burning and by dawn
burnt down

                         (I want to wake at the wheel still driving
somehow changed, want you there beside me
as the road unwires like a heartline, lilting
and we near another elsewhere
want you there at the wheel, at the wheel
I still believe
for as long as it turns
I can clutch the sun I can steer and
brake time to a hold ——)

These times I still believe in every poem the road gave me
though at daybreak they shrink away
like a distance every sign, and the road

that seemed by night a bare arm
unbroached by any watch, and reaching
ah, into dawn, emerges

Mondayed ——
bone-beige ——
manacled with quartz ——

                              a scar in the suburbs
of a clock-skulled place.

To Our Eyes the Blind Man

To our eyes the blind man's lover was ugly
when she would guide him each evening, patient,
past dirty windows and the slandering eyes
of our neighbourhood — she never tired
of the gauntlet, the grins, the whispering
gathered schoolboys or their poised
silence so much worse than whispering. . . .

And there I was with the others — the lean one,
laughing — while streetlamps at the butt of long
late-summer days grew bright and spotlit
the two of them: scapegoats in a circus ring
without roof or limit, so our laughter
leapt free, grew up as it hardened
into the walls and streets and crowds we knew as cities. . . .

Ugly, the boys sang, and I sang, but he clutched
her hand so tight, so tight it seemed
he was the one guiding her into the sweet
dark city of his love — free
from the bitter half-lit boroughs of the seeing.

Elegy as a Message Left on an Answering Machine

Hello, you've reached 542-0306. I'm unable to answer the phone just now, but just leave a message after the beep and I'll be sure to return your call.

Goodbye for now

Won't bother waiting up for you
to get back to me on this one. Waste of time.
My dime
in a bar by the water, your factory-new

answering machine is —— like anything bereaved —— still
full of your words, the waves
of your voice, the nervous laugh that gave us,
sometimes, "cause" to laugh. And which we now miss. Well,

human nature. I say Fuck my own. I own
up: this stinks. Too late
to erase all the crap, a watergate
of gossip, off-hand words, no time to phone-

in those last minute changes, additions, to say
what we find so impossible to say ——
I find. So cut all this *can't*
come to the phone right now cant, I don't

buy it, I figure you're in there somewhere, still
screening your calls, you
secretive bastard, pick up the phone right now if you
would hear a friend. Don't stall,

don't, like me. Thinking
there's time, there's still time enough, or rather
not thinking enough. Now look, I'm not sure whether
the executors will be disconnecting

you —— your line —— tomorrow (nurses, almost, pulling closed
the green curtain and tearing
out of your torso the drips and plugs and electrodes
to leave you drifting

with that astronaut in the film
who squirms awhile, signals some last, frantic word
then spins away into the void) ——
that's why I'm here. Sky's clear tonight, by the way, calm

the wind, the water. Not sure really
why I called ——
gesture of a drunk old
friend and ally.

Anyway it was pretty good
for a second or two, to
get through,
Tom,

goodbye.

Conversation in a Gallery

The exhibition halls were deserted. Occasional guards
dozed awkwardly at their posts
like unfinished statuary. It seemed it hardly
mattered what I stole or took the trouble to deface.

In a viewing room I thought I'd almost
stumbled on another visitor: it was actually a life-
sized statue, set in place
before a wall of staring portraits. Art

paying attention to art. Life
imitates nothing without our eyes, and finally ghosts
all we do with a fine film of soil
or dust —— and yet

as at a conference of adepts (art-
scholars, psychologists and the collectors
of china or rare insects) there is this traffic
between dignified stone heads or heads in dry oil

in a dialect no one else knows, which is therefore
silent. Silent, as this gallery is now
with its long row of reluctant jurors
who are going to have to accept the coming verdict

     and really you would like to know

how for so long these dessicated gazes drew you
into a fool's auction, and sold you
their hourglass shares of time-
past and time-future
in exchange for all your currency
     —— in exchange for perfect rhymes and resonant conceits
that might survive the moment or the era
the inconvenience of, say, a lover or a child is
nothing, they whispered
     for what seemed a long time

I paid attention to their words
while the wordless trials of a lover turned the room
into a ghost-gallery of cases, closed,
and I paid and I paid and I paid.

An Elegy, Years After Sarah

So her ceiling a map of stars. First time we made love
late afternoon late winter, and after as she slept
how her room fogged up with dusk
and paper stars she'd stuck up there in childhood
came out in strange constellations
and I missed the earth
till her room was night her breath deepening the stars
cooling down: I said *come closer* and her eyes
—— half-open, flashing back whatever light there was —— went out.

Dylan's Source

Green as a dungeon
                    he was chained
   to the rain's ramshackling
                        spirits
                                    sailed
      over hills of his saying

         and tumbled
                    drunk as a gull
                              to the sea's sweet breadth ——

At death
                        they carried him like a king
      to a new dominion

                  his grinning lip
                              flecked amber
               with a drop of drink
                                 the shade and ringing
                     tone of rusted
                              chain

Triolet

Confide in the darkness that inspires
like death. Breath whitens the winter panes.
In streets below your window, scattered wires
confide in the darkness that inspires.
Night is vital. Void desires
return to soil like dead-end lanes.
Confide in the darkness that inspires
like death. Breath whitens the winter panes.

Psalm: Hands of the Beautiful Swimmers

Three friends in the ocean call me over
and over the flats at low tide   I see them
wade into a future of waves, white sails
and freighters, calling clockwise, bound away
for other berths.

                Makes migrants of them all, the sea: ex-
friends and fathers, lovers, children —— lost
to ticking riptides, drifting off
like shorebirds tarred in a slick, as wind
shifts and the shouted words reshape themselves
in memory.

              They'll never be so beautiful
as now, their gold bodies going down
into the sea like minor suns, their fingers
frail and waving as a sun's last rays;
and here on the last shores of the day
a watcher weeps for having never seized
the hands of the beautiful swimmers.

A. D.

a dialogue of hemispheres

. . . *art owes its ongoing evolution to
the Apollonian-Dionysian duality, just
as the propagation of the species hangs on
the duality of the sexes, with their ongoing
conflicts and occasional acts of reunion.*

— Nietzsche, *The Birth of Tragedy*

Prologue

Divorce was a hooded, shadowy caller
armed with a briefcase instead of a scythe.
Back then he paid house calls to so many
families in our neighbourhood
so come nightfall, bedtime, the brittle, bare
staircase by my room would screech and
jitter and rumble with my fear he would come,
had come, to see us.
                    He never called.
                              Yet the stairs
kept creaking, twelve teeth of a saw, jig-
sawing the soft place where I dreamed
into a labyrinth of forks and junctures, seeing my father
was English, my mother Greek
and so different, and though they gave no sign
they would ever ask Him in, I was afraid

                    that one night gliding past us on his rounds
he would sniff out the hybrid, oddball
energies of our house
and with his empty X-ray sockets, home in
on dotted lines of tension in the walls
and with bony finger pick the locks
        — and my parents, loud
in argument or love, wouldn't hear a thing
till he'd swept up behind and his briefcase had
sprung open like a cobra's jaws
and our lives were vacuumed in.

                         Home
for us was no womb but a crucible, a carnival
of masks, mouths carved in every mood
a melting pot full of hail and grapeleaves
that would never boil down to one — to nothing —
or feed the hooded guy.

                    Home —
where any table and page is, and I pen them
together in a room again: close the paper
door of the notebook and leave them
face to face,

                    still talking —

Elegy, Apollo I

Du mußt dein Leben ändern

As the cockpit filled with fire it must have seemed
the rockets were erupting backwards, as if to drive
the ship's alloys back down into ore-crammed
veins underground, the astronauts in their cave

of circuitry and radium shot drifting to the north
as atoms, ash for gravity and the draughts
to reconcile with their home country, earth.
Last night, that nightmare you have where jets

like reckless sons are shuttling from the skies
skywriting this: you have to. Change. *Du mußt.*
The dashboard's face of glowing dials and gauges

like the calm, measured mask of Apollo, fused
to madness, melts, its data burning with the eyes
of tigers starving in tin-can cages.

Dionysus & the Fire

Never arm a man who can't dance

—— Irish Proverb

Tonight
Dubrovnik burning
& one time Lhasa, London in the blitz
& last year in the Gardens of Babylon, just wilted
women's shawls
widowed with ash, with atoms of a daughter, son
fresh-weaned from this breast of a planet
left hanging

       & the war?
the war is as good as won
       & the brain?
the brain is a smart bomb
         dance

   Each conflagration
outside in the world, the prime time
world out there: a fire we denied the body
   Each blast in the underground   each rite of arson
a votive flame to the mortal, smothered
in the rubble of the brain's walls at Dubrovnik
in the stubble of the pasture where the mass grave grins
& Baghdad
Baghdad burning
had we danced

as if that would have solved it all
like a quick howl in the backwoods, brother,
like a dip in the Jordan, like a guru's
swiss-bank-shrewd prescriptions
    but still, I do want to sing
though how can I sing?
                    I do,
                        of the heart's genius
drunk with dreaming:
                    dancing
you burst from the cage of your form
a wildcat of air whose stripes are flame from the ducts
of a shuttle, exploding, a bird
a serpent egged from the heart
whose genius you seem   you are   your breath a steam-cobra
        coiling up
through Edens of January air, in the alley
where you drop your books your paintbox briefcase toolbox
        bulletproofvest
or maybe just dream it?
                    dreaming this:

        the white fruits of the snow pulped by dancers to a wine
                of slush & water, the two-step
        Cartesian shuffle & the crippling, long, hob-
                        nailing gravity of Apollo's prohibition
            washed away
                        & the clerks in herring-bone funeral files
                    noosed in matching neckties for how many million
        man-hours on the gallows of habit
                            cut down
                    almost dancing, their fibres forgetful
                        but catching the hang of it again, again &
                        bursting from the cage of their form

& you may be dreaming but what seems sheer Dali now
is the dailyness, midwinter, how the downturned & trodden
faces drugged, adrowse to their freedom
& the fabulous dowry of another night
another hour
sleep on, leaden, & you with them, as the Sony
pokes its smoking barrel into your cell, & the too-late
news fires in with footage LIVE
FROM GROUND ZERO
over there
Guernica Lhasa Hiroshima Dilli
flat for ages & a picnic table in the wilderness
turned to glass, where colonels like beautiful
boys round a mountain pool peer down
and lunch on their own reflections
                                (& the face

the face is mine)

                    & the war?
                            the war is as good as won
                    & the brain?
                            the brain is a smart bomb

                                        dance

1

Birthday

Mornings, the sunbeams' flowing escalator drew up
at your mother's door, drew up
your eyes and weaned them from the damp
verandah while, nine months new, you crawled
under the window where your mother baked. Called

and called to at ten months, you pressed on, turtled
down steps to the garden —— bold turtle
without a shell, back damp
with dew from drooping poppies, as if wet
from the egg, and your mother must have felt

there, a tugging, a pang at the navel
as if the scalpel never sheared your navel
as you pulled away from her into the damp
and drying world, a third eye in the belly you both
once saw from —— when? —— welling damp with

sweat, fear's scalpel at the heart
sawing, stabbing . . . A month older and her heart
could hardly stand the laughter as you in your damp
bulging trousers tried to stand
until, for a moment, you *stood* —— and never mind

that two steps later you tumbled in the sun
or that a month later in the autumn sun
you'd still be falling —— to her, at the door, hands damp
with frosting, you'd roamed beyond all reeling back
though even now she recalls you for the cake

      she holds in the doorway, calling!
            calling! while years away in the roses you break
              and bury her heart in the garden,
                        to grow.

Portrait of a Father

I dreamed his head was floating on the sea
and said these words   *Leave the forest*
for the sun's shore, for Apollo   the body
is a hallowed cannibal: noon is best,

quit the cult of the pulse and the wine-beams
bleeding like war from the moon's barrel. (The rest
was swallowed with a roar, as the sea
opened, whale-wide.

                    I woke up.)
                        In other dreams

he's carried out past saving on his own brain-waves,
body blue as an embryo, a glacier, in a blank sea
never free of signs: the passing sails

hold sonnets, the horizon electric with heart-waves
hums, and the eye is a diving bell plunged through the sea
to where the sun's silver machinery fails.

Slow Lightning

(a scholar as child)

Four years brought a sunrise of memory
in a beam of light descending a stairwell
lined with ancestral faces. Now I see them, baffled
under glass, trapped behind iron
bars of sunlight from the forge
of a star much older, cooler than their own.
Their lips and hair, pale sepia skin
all like my father's, flickering
on the memory's screen, the blank back of the skull
where I still see the door
of his study swing ajar, his body
in the threshold a guardian, his teeth
grinning like a chain of keys.

And when I went in: dim shelves refuting the faint
light trailing me from the door, desk of rosewood,
broad-backed chair, so many books my head spun
when I tried to count them. And trying to reckon
with the room's seductions I went in again
and again, a moth caught by the spidery light
of print on bindings, or pulled
by the vortex from a bonfire of volumes
burning in a city square.
                              When he caught me
he said nothing, led me out with soft compositor's hands
more used to a book's brittle spine —— and the door behind us
shut like a cover. So we stood outside
in the cold passage, hand-in-hand, and as I grew
to fill his absence he held me fast, those portraits
fading, my father gone, and still
on the carpeted stairway
the sunbeam
fell,
        slow lightning.

"Lightning bolt in the blackout . . . "

Lightning bolt in the blackout, gone.
In time all things will be explained.
The mind is a drunk, stumbling for the phone:
lightning, wrung out of darkness. Gone ——
that lone skiff seen leaving the bay
in the brief flash, as the brain's hand
in shadow, gropes, and a dial-tone
fills the room like the hurricane
clearing its throat. To speak. To say
some phrase electric as the dawn
or lightning in the dark; a feigned
flash of day in the blackout, bone
in X-ray glimpsed, then gone ——
all things in time will be explained.

Lightning bolt in the blackout ——

Haiku: Weather Station, Baffin Island

Cold report of these
  Gloved hands slapped for warmth —— the sound
    Of one hand clapping.

In Heraclitus' City

Begin like sisters with fingers linked, the city
and the sea, quayed where the marble street would end
2000 years back, and every year since then
for the length of a long bone the sea has been

crawling off and moss darkening the dead-end
cobbles with a caul of green, so now the jetty,
broken, reaches — seems to reach — out to a receding,
far-off fingertip of the Aegean. These hours

that sand down faces, bury vows in desert graves, and send
sisters to scattered time zones, cities, bereave us
of our harbours; in the tumbled senate, wind

has the last civil word, while melodramatic above the ruins
the theatre spreads out its great robed arms
and after twenty centuries can say nothing.

The Thief

We brought him down from the hill with the sun
hot on our shoulders, filed like apostles
past the woodlot's edge, into flourishing shade
where limbs of Lebanon cedar touched him

and left him there among deadfall, folding
the quick, dead hands, knowing his last escape
would go unwitnessed in the isolate
eye of the orchard, after the hawkers' cries,

the clamour and swearing, the brute barter
a cloak of noise that covered him. Fallen
here among olives, the soft inviolate shade
must have troubled him, surely, or would have, if. . . ?

        It was bad enough to be ignored at the end,
buckling, splayed like a plummeting angel
in the hot wind, his stammerings swallowed
by the mob's roar; after a lifetime of furtive silence

he must have had something to say to them.
But the congregation hadn't come to hear
and the guards went on to the day's main draw
while their cold carpentry did the trick.

        And yet, though nobody listened
he must have found the word —— we saw him shudder
and cough, groan, struggle to gesture
but there were nails through his crooked hands

and feet, the barest motion was a trial, the sun
a mass of molten gold. Late afternoon. Long after
the other thief had flagged, and the slender man
on the middle cross, crowned with thistles

grew too weak to amuse the crowd, storm clouds
clustered on the skyline, there was talk of rain
and the crowd thinned before a last fugitive
breath escaped him. As early darkness curtained in

and the dying prophet pleaded with the air
we freed the fallen thief from his cross
and brought him down from the hill.
      We left him lying in the fragrant deadfall

of an orchard, turned, filed away
in the fallen dark along aisles of olive trees
ripe with rain, yet felt on our shoulders
a warmth, like sun: the word on his tongue, still flickering.

For You, Without Words

He took her on night-buses and trains
so in the shuddering dark when sleep
was a far-off destination, he breathed
in the mouth of his memory, till the clouding panes

shrouded his eyes and the landscape, and the window
was a wall, a frieze, unfinished in her absence, empty . . .
    To argue with her again, scheme and vow
and laugh and lie down in her arms, how could he

dream the pulsing clichés of distance and return
could ever age or weaken? Yet he lost the right words
again and again. High above him the peaks

in perfect silence kept on carving their epochs
of fossil and stone, and still the night-winds
at the frozen sill hissed only   *Ah* ——

Fragment

Lovers on trains and buses
never see the landscape passing, for the streams
of hair above seats ahead (the hair of lovers
half-forgotten); for the hands
of Sarah, five years dead, in two small clouds
above the sun; for the round
of their own reflections, Narcissized
there in the window's
dark tarn ——

Annotation of a Fragment

from *The Scholar's Collected Works*

Let there remain beside success[1] and the homage of colleagues[2]
Coffee in styrofoam cups[3] and my wife[4]
Who waited beside me thirty years, silent[5] over steaming
Mugs for mail to come[6]
this:[7] the fragrance her breasts held
after we'd walked in woods behind the college[8] the way
her fingers flickered in sleep and maybe
I should have closed my books that one time
she rushed into my room full of warm breath & language & leaned
over to say the word[9] but saw I was somewhere far away
& never did[10]

1 – By the time this fragment was composed The Scholar (Dr John Hartnell) had published six books of criticism and countless articles. The critical volumes, including his acclaimed *A.E. Housman, Sylvia Plath, and the Prosody of Subtle Joy*, were thematically unorthodox and at times controversial, but always prominent and influential.

2 – By the time of his death, Hartnell's reputation had achieved Messianic proportions. Dean Howard Cackley (1904-1979) once remarked that "The Scholar's colleagues typically behave[d] more like disciples than peers."

3 – During the last decade of his life it was Hartnell's avowed hope that the department would allot a certain sum for the purchase of ceramic coffee mugs. On several occasions he imparted to colleagues his "profound fear" that styrofoam, like other "products of convenience," was "quietly poisonous" and gradually eroded the intellect and constitution. He left behind several pages of notes toward an article on the subject.

4 – When he was thirty-one, in the same year he completed his doctorate, Hartnell married Helen Tara Stevens, another PhD. The marriage seems to have been turbulent and troubled almost from the start. At departmental gatherings The Scholar and his spouse were frequently heard to exchange erudite and highly intertextual insults; on one unforgettable occasion she announced distinctly that he had not slept with her "for several semesters." The couple had no children.

5 – The marriage, characterized as it was by a certain physical reserve, was also notoriously silent. The biographers observe that when Helen Hartnell entertained company her husband would lock himself in the lavatory with his books, emerging only when dinner was served. After the meal he would insist the coffee be served in styrofoam cups.

6 – The Scholar was an impatient correspondent. Herman Moberley, who delivered his mail for over two decades, confirms that in the early years Hartnell was apt to lurk by the front door — or, in fair weather, behind the azaleas — and then upon Herman's appearance pounce forth in his bathrobe, ready to seize the daily mail. Years later Hartnell would see his own behaviour as a "juvenile manifestation" of the "Western tendency to watch the offing, to wait for news and portents from distant places and seize *them* instead of the day itself." He would be embarrassed, moreover, recalling how he had liked to analyse his wife's correspondence searching for flaws in grammar and spelling.

7 – Here the shift in tone and style, from professorially contemplative to purely lyrical, is remarkable for its suddenness and apparent spontaneity. The biographers risibly submit that "the reference must be to a woman Dr Hartnell knew before his marriage, as his courtship was conducted with chaste propriety — even his love letters being drafted on departmental stationery and typed by a secretary." They hazard further that the woman may have been "one of his students during his tenure as a doctoral candidate and research assistant in Toronto (1947-50)" (Quayle et al., 766).

It seems far more likely, given the time of their writing, that the lines were composed for and about his dying wife Helen.

8 – The woodlot behind the college was destroyed in 1961 to make room for the new humanities wing. Perhaps ironically Hartnell's office from that point on was in the heart of what had been the "woods."

9 – Could Hartnell be referring here to Joyce's "word known to all men"? It is impossible to be sure. The biographers' wild surmise that "the woman was simply hoping for an extension on a paper" is clearly out of line; since the woman in question is surely Helen, the "word" may have been something simpler, more domestic —— a request that Hartnell come to dinner, perhaps, or pick up the phone.

10 – The "ending" is enigmatic, and the lack of final punctuation implies the piece is unfinished, a fragment. For nowhere else, whether in manuscript, typescript, or notes, does The Scholar forego the final period. The omission may of course be accidental, a reflection of the deep fatigue and violent madness that plagued him through his final weeks; indeed it is possible it was these very lines he was working on at the time of his death.

If there is any indication at all of how the finished work might have appeared, it may lie in these similarly uncharacteristic and thus possibly related lines found scribbled in the margin of his *Collected Donne*:

> *she did never and elsewhere I was seen*
> *crying say the word*
> *say the word only say*
> *language and wombwarm breath of full*
> *room into me rushed for a time she did say to me say*
> *nothing, love*
> *close this book).*

Rewriting the Dead

What we glimpse of her now is less
than the frozen trickle of light from a star
extinct since the Pharaohs' age

yet flickering. Every hour the familiar eyes
get fainter, the form less clear; the living
come to revise her words, like cousins

contesting a will, and claiming
who she loved most, most favoured —— who she failed
to praise —— who she failed. The dead

are a newfound planet, drifting,
distant as Neptune's moons, but colonized
quickly, gridded with myth, their bones

embellished like the relics of saints ——
each breath they're less themselves and more
like satellites in a galaxy, born

of need and speculation. Because we must
we rewrite the dead —— bind them in silence and dust-
jackets of soil, of pine. Soon enough their souls

become too frail to slip
the gravity of defining words, and fail
to check our sloppy captions. So they don't point out

how we absolve them of their being
and replace them, soon, the way a stellar
hologram might be flashed on the sky

at the moment the Pharaohs' star blinks out.

Glosa

I wept when I remembered
How often you and I
Had tired the sun with talking
And sent it down the sky
—— Kallimachus, fl. N. Africa c. 350 BC

You were careful, at the first brush of the wing,
not to put anyone out. The pain and numbness
kicked in at dawn; you waited till 9:15 —— not 9 ——
to call your doctor. He told you
Heart attack. Get yourself down to Hotel Dieu, Emergency,
        fast. Tom,
you walked. You walked the mile and a bit —— you lumbered,
really, side to side, because, you said, your legs
felt leaden, your head light, your heart tightening like a
        drawstring sack.
Who held the strings? For three days none of us heard.
I wept when I remembered

how you'd tried not to put us out, how we only
found you by chance, then abashed you with visits, vases
filled with the clover and scilla flourishing then
in your own, overgrown yard. Mild, you said ——
you said the experts pronounced it mild, and you fine.
You looked fine. Just cut the booze, you said, the bacon
        and eggs. Try
try to remember your pills, all seventeen of them
though you only mentioned a couple, and we only
found the others later. Now, looking back, I'm surprised by
how often you and I

did get together, despite everything, the busyness, the dead-
lines down every hall, like lasers in a rigged house; the way a
             single man
comes to cave in on himself, like a house untended, his ego
an armchair in the wreckage, the staved-in
windows blocked and jagged, so the hand tendered in or out
never quite arrives. Yet we did get together and I managed, walking
beside you through a city of fractures (between prison and prep-
             school,
earth/river/lake) to see the patient friend in you break
surface in your eyes, though it seemed you weren't listening,
had tired the sun with talking,

were ready to retire to that armchair, where no babbling
novice irked you with his   wooden table talk. Well
sure. I know the feeling. How you didn't — didn't seem to —
listen. Tom,
             listen now: last night I dreamed a tree was growing
out of your house, a dozen boughs through every door, each window,
             scraping
clear through the skylight, as scilla will blaze up through an eye-
socket in the earth. There were leaves, and the delicate skeletons
of small birds hung in wind-chimes off the boughs. Their marrow
was music, like yours now — song. Off the cliff of my tongue I made
             the music fly

                    and sent it down the sky.

A Sonnet for the Body

(a deathbed dream)

Helen, the fields! The fields are full of sparks, of fire-
flies that dart and glitter like goldfish in a dark pool
under the moon, the full moon! Helen, you know that lull
when the reader puts down the book, and the entire
world is out of focus for a glance? So a man who reads too much
might lose the cities and the land, but Helen, tonight
the fields are full of stars! My eyes are set like gems in the bright
orbits of a young man's skull, on a body bound over the high grass where
        cicadas chant a path, and the birch-
ribbed forest pulsing with heat and hungering
night enfolds me. Look, the mirror lies! Turn down your bed! The nails
        of your fingers fling
fire in the moonlight and I am back from the forest. Heated
beams through the magnifying glass of your window show this sheeted
bed an open book, untouched, and our bodies have something to say,
to sing. Long lines for the monocled eye of the moon! A sonnet
        for the body!

You Slept Better Then

Masks I shed and left by the roadside
share this view with me tonight.
(Blue hills, and beyond the snowcloud
an inkling of the lake.)

Here's one that fit all right ——
I wore it sometimes when I loved you, and stowed it
away like a weapon, loaded
whenever you slept.

You never knew. You slept better then.

And if you felt something brittle, break
just barely, just under the skin
when you touched my lips, or kept
kissing and kissing my eyes, you   never did let on.

Bone, I would have told you. Bone.

The Bed *(a letter)*

A week before boarding ferries
for separate ports, we found a bed
in the orchard above the inn,
abandoned. How many falls?
Dead leaves curled together
by the headboard, wind
snoring in the olive trees.
That mattress, gutted, where mice
had hollowed out their feather rooms —
their catacombs.
                    Beneath the road
the gorge was filled with the greening
relics of buses, cars; dark shrines
roosted above us like ravens
in the hillside.

And the rain. Did I forget
to mention it? Well,
we've had some more.

Just yesterday I saw it fall
through a bone-dry morning
onto islands off the coast.

Poet with Sedna, Goddess of the Sea

Dive through the green sea-ice
of this statue's eyes, the staring
soapstone airholes where seals break

burning surface, and you're adrift
in cyan gorges, spun by the cold
amniotic currents of a womb fired

by lunar rays. We emerge out of cold
we return to the cold
intercostal abyss between stars, the Arctic

night an Easter sun will not unfreeze ——
      The woman under the sea, they sing, is
hunkering in eyeless caverns, spying from the air-

locks of drifting bergs, and from channels
snapping closed in the fjord; her eyes
in glare-ice strain from a roadside

on the long drive south. Bare ribs, open window
on an August night, fireflies at the screen,
and a man with a carving pressed to his temple

for the green cold the stone retains.

Epitaph, Unfinished

From a two-line fragment, dyslexically scrawled in the notebook of a crewman from the disastrous Franklin Expedition of 1845-48[?]. The notebook was found by a search party, in 1854, beside the remains of an unidentified sailor who had been involved in the crew's doomed march south towards the mainland.

Oh Death whare is thy sting, the grave
At Comfort Cove for who has any doubt now . . . the dyer
Said . . . Whare is thy victory

In cairns by a seacoast none sails, whare the point
In nought returning now the year's Spring
When Kings go forth, our ship a Jonah in the white jaws of

What Season this? What Easter
& the ship unmanned behind by God I
saw some slip bone-anchor through a wheezing

porthole of the sea; saw souls so trudged by the cross of labour
Rope-burn Wind-burn Eyes blind at barely Noon
each body, —— lean —— a sundial aimed at
  aimed at

How sting of gravel horned us, boots
stuffed for the storm with pages, teared
from prayer-books *I shall not want*
Here in a horde of poor devils in the wilderness, whare Christ
tempts &

taunts us
Ah
one sprig of larksong & gladly I
should slow as my ink & wander a

way from the dying lines:

alone. to the parched hymn of
Is it grey, gunbarrel
breakers beating Judgement?

See

see how they Fall each frothing crest by

Christ a palm a Finger

pointing into,

2

two by two in the ark of
the ache of it

—— Denise Levertov

Graveyard in the North Country

for Jeff

Under the earth the bones grow lonely
abandoned by their flesh, and loved ones
who no longer come to june the gravestones
with green roses, or sweep away the dust.

August, and summer dies away: voices
among the tombs grow faint: the patter
of feet between stooped crosses softening
to autumn rain. All Souls, then the muffling snow

made us dream of drawing our losses
from leaden soil to warmer beds, but
they would not have known our hands, they forget
themselves, and we are dead to them

though living.
                    How is it, in the bleak
midwinter light, when monuments engrave
sundial shadows on the pale face
of the snow, and blind bones lie stargazing

at galaxies of fossils — how is it we can live
with how we forget them, with our urgent
desertion, the way the graves
sink deeper with time? How even in spring

when warm winds furrowed with seeds
of wildflower and waking earth compel you,
faithful, back to the freshness, the church-
grounds stay empty, no visits are made?

A stone-faced sun and moon hold vigil
in their patient wake, but do not mourn.
The stars turn a mass of blind eyes
to the earth; at sundown, skies grow deep

like a grave.
                    Under the earth, the bones
grow lonely, abandoned by their flesh, and loved ones
who no longer come to summer stones
with green roses, or sweep away the dust.

Graveyard in the North Country, Again

Through a telescope of bone: nebulae
of fossils, shale
atmospheres under a field in winter *can you hear me*
hear me still   where the bones grow
lonely as brown, brittle grass (but bones
never do grow "lonely"

no)

& if the dead could dream
& we overheard:

> *a door into the earth door closing behind us*
> *a way out a ways beneath winter neither here nor*
> *elsewhere over thunderheads of clay hailing down*
> *free of small talk free of in-trays out-trays*
> > *& the clock-*
> *punching sun "by salaries*
> *betrayed" & sold &*
> *sucked dry of all our currency in this bargain*
> *basement of the*

Through the fine scope of a finger's bone: cells and
neutrons iridescing
like the fireflies we saw one dusk
hovering in the hollowed
ribs of a dead horse, by the fence
of an Indian graveyard in the Rockies

ah,

if the dead could drink
& our words were rain:

> *I loved you like a field without fences*
> *filled by the mountain's galloping shadow.*
> *Every quarter of the wind that rolled*
> *like a gust of forgetting through the senses*
> *drives me toward you. Each hour of broken road*
> *I choked down with the bile of custom*
> *crumbles into dust with the dumb wisdom*
> *of the elements, is spread apart by weeds,*
> *enveloped by the steady rockfall.*
> > *Years now, roofless, drunk with the rains*
> *at the treeline where only trails make choices,*
> *we're still climbing together to the col*
> *as your bones sink deeper roots into the plains*
> *and spur the dust of Assiniboine horses.*

Hikers

It's always best to walk behind
other hikers on the trail, or follow
tracks into thick forest, where narrow
crooks and blinds distract the eye

so the moment's stride is all you know
and the woods conceal the coming rise ——
that sheer grade, like a sleepless night,
always close to ending. But what if it showed ——

if we could picture the paths of our life
scrambling over scree, up the treeless meadows
and the balding ridge, until the body is slowed
by thin air and age, and draws near the divide?

    Much better for some to come behind
through the blind, dense forest, with heads bowed.

Walker

Sometimes walking home in late afternoon
the look of a lane catching the light will catch
your eye and you might pause at the head
of the lane and looking down it watch
shadows crawl into nooks and tin pails or the tint
of spent sun on a red brick garage
and maybe a boy kicking shards of grit or a clenched
can over hot gravel. You might walk up that lane
by gaping sheds, cars rusting and gates, flies
floating like dust from old carpets until
you stop in a path of sun, then, turning,
take it between buildings.
                         In the shadows there
as white shirts and tattered
sheets beat at the light
breeze, a tended dooryard will appear
to your left. Unexpected
you will pause a minute or so then
go to the door and knock as the air
of late August insinuates
something, hear the clink of cutlery and vague
voices from kitchen windows where half-
remembered silhouettes resolve and vanish, in the eaves
the scream and flutter of birds
in the neighbouring street an engine starting
    and somewhere the slam of a door, shut.

Psalm: For the Wind & the Shield Country

The wind is my shepherd, and I must walk
Where it drives me until day's end.
It guides me into barren hills
More beautiful than gardens, at dark
It leads me to lie
Under sheets of rain, it feeds me
The warm wafer of the sun
Steaming from dawn's embers. I am drawn down
By the wind's fingers to waters
That are never still, my staff
And compass are the living boughs, the leaves
My roof, my shifting floor,
                              and I must live
Like the mountain, briefly
And always, in wide
Mansions of the wind.

A Psalm, on Second Thought

       I'm not afraid of taking this harp
down from the willow
to sing —— though no one
trusts song much any more, or the singer ——
       and sometimes this harp is a hacksaw, my fibres
pulsating to notes
a living ash might make when carved
my words are warrants
my metre martial
my pacifist slogan a summons to war
       I've confused, at times, orders
for order, I've psalmed orchards
loaded with lush plump fruit and not
the prison walls behind, I've chanted
Carmanesque Shield Country isles as acid
suds censored the far shore, said *barren*
hills more beautiful than gardens —— ignoring
the tools or tailings that
made them so.
            I'm not afraid of easing this harp
out of the limbs of the dying
willow to sing, but who can sing, and not become
the laureate of a state
of legislated greed?
                And if my tongue forget?

                         I'm afraid
at times,
       of taking this harp
down from the dead
willow to sing

—— and hung their harps on the willows, yearning
by the waters of a strange land.
                              How can we sing
"psalms for the wind & the shield country"
as bodies burn in a lake of fire
by the rivers of Babylon, & the sea
gives up its dead to slicks & sewage, & the atmosphere
in its breathing sac round the planet
blackens like a miner's lung?
        Walt Whitman in wartime, crying
Must I change my triumphant songs?
Must I indeed learn to chant the cold dirges of the baffled?
And sullen hymns of defeat?
        Sweet earth burning with battle & greed
how can we sing? Voices chilled
as the coffin passes, how can we sing?
In a time of glibness and disbelief
when beauty is disbelieved, & love, & leaders
in a parliament of lies whisper
mechanical lies, who can sing?
                        Yet the stars in the dying river
tonight, so clear, the radium wind on my skin,

                                even now you hear them,

feel them,
        sing:

in a valley of tailings
                              the wind
                 was my ward, orphaned, my failing
garden of air, &
                          goodness &
                                        mercy

                 will surely

                              all the days of my

55

Nightfall in the Gulf, January '91

Moon's face droops down
  pale as radium from a
    noose of furious stars

Nakunaru

In the Japanese language *to die*
is to become invisible, to be lost
to go missing
               so when Hideyuki Murata disappeared
in the August blast, scoured
from a street in the core of Nagasaki
               haunting the upper air as atoms of heat
or energy mingled with cinders
               of his wife and children, winnowing
down into fields along the coast

               So when he disappeared, it seemed
his language had already prepared
a vocabulary to deal with his loss

and when Hideyuki went
with his 75 years, he took
these things with him:

the peculiar bluegreen
his eyes made of bays east of Shimabara
when he first fished there with his uncle
the way the paddy-field by his house
had smelled in the summer heat, of rice
steaming, newly cooked
his mother's voice calling him to supper
a freak snow one April, melted down
by noon, the sweet
stab of a crabapple
biting into his tongue, a best friend shot beside him
at Mukden, 1905
his first monsoon his father dead
and a woman kissed him ——

and old eyes noting in wind
over the harbour
a single silver gleam —— a seagull maybe
flying inland, catching the early light

and disappearing
with a clap of thunder
into remarkable clouds

Takayama *(a dream in Japanese)*

You feel, so far inland,
    in a seabird's midnight cry
        the loss of a baby daughter.

❋❋❋

By the river, where paper houses
perch on stilts like herons
in a rising tide, I sit
and dangle feet in currents
white as milk with melted snow, and wait
till the river rises through my emptiness, fills
my belly my heart my breasts, and breaks
in ocean brine from my eyes.

❋❋❋

Why did you leave me
for the open sky?
Clouds rise, too,
but in a fall of snow
return to the earth.

Beloved

A china doll speeds toward me out of the dark. Mid-air. Out of the crawlspace into the room where my daughter sleeps. Goes on sleeping, on the sofa, while the floorboards judder and the walls groan. I've drummed my fist on the floorboards to draw the baby out, howled a challenge, sworn so obscenely my throat clamped on the words and they belched out deformed and foreign, my nape, my backbone hackling, chilled —— and now bursting from the crawlspace the pale child flies straight at me, my arms stretching hard to take it embrace it or block its flight and throttle it like a rabid stray, but it scuds through my hands with green marble eyes ivory teeth and skin of cadaverous china, surging, smashing into my face, my skull. My open eyes. Shattered.

Stone Mountain Elegy

for Chris

In April, winds off the glacier
blow between stones of a graveyard
in the mountains. Here your mother is
buried, and you've asked us to go,
come, leave flowers, clean the site, bring

news that all is —— what? Peaceful, I suppose.
In its place, not vandalized, not quite
vanished. And everything is all right ——
everything is fine. We leave a vase,
clean the plot, bow faces, pace

among stones, but as the others head
for the fence it strikes me I'm afraid
to let you know what a small thing
a stone is in the mountains. No
matter how tall, how elaborate,

it's shadowed, always, by the great
shrugged shoulder of the range —— I guess
when you were here you must have seen?
I could tell you, too, how faults
in the mountain spell out names in snow

(names no one can ever read, or say)
but you must know that too. When
was the last time you travelled west?
Ten years? Twenty? How they pass . . .

And the small stones seem to whisper now
        what was it kept you away?

Stone Mountain Postscript

Time in a country where the hour
                              before dawn is the hour
       when rivers run loudest
                   when the quartz clocks in every greenwich
pause
                         when the glacier like a shunting train
    in a boneyard of cloud & chasms   slips
                its midnight inch
                              & dark erodes

        the graveyard's dead inscriptions

                    & the stones are stones again

                                                    Old friend,

I remember you mentioning now
how one time years ago in that graveyard under Rundle
(the biggest headstones not even foothills
in those mountains!) you were out with a woman
walking —— your lover? —— when you both saw
lying on her back in the sun by the fence
with hat & arm flung over her eyes
your mother

& as you paused there in the heat, & glacial
cold stole up your spine, your mother
pale as a queen of sleeping marble
sat up suddenly, as if a nightmare, breathing,
had just brought her back, her eyes
pried open & seeing fiercely
nothing at all —

                not your mother's eyes at all
of course, the woman younger, a stranger — a tourist
in town for the day?
                Of course —

So as the stranger, embarrassed,
lay back down, her face freezing
back into marble, the two of you walked away, you thinking
you'd have to tell your mother
how somehow you'd thought —

                      how somehow you'd wondered

what you have to wonder eventually
somewhere
in the rainfall of high graveyards
in the hour before dawn
when the clock's arms are splayed like a sleeper's
& the river runs loudest, outgrieving
even the wind
piping through monuments, the rockfall & the last
dying words of the train:

you!

you!

you

you?

& the stones are stones again

A Triolet, Abandoned

Caged birds sing sweetest
—— Richard Wilbur

A bird is a poem
that speaks of the end of cages
—— Patrick Lane

Trust in the silence that succeeds
Each breath. Death cleanses the soul like bone.
Words are prisms, are prisons that creeds
And theorists construct from the air down: with guards
At every gap and words
In horizontal bars: the lines
 (maybe) of a triolet, you outside keyless in the cold
When what I wanted most —— needed
  most —— was to pull you in through the bars like someone
sick to death of solitary and wanting
    something more than this alien symmetry
        —— wanting conversation   some Saturday your good friend
      outside doorless in summer yet the dialogue
        is a warm winter room, where the words
                    resonate and wrestle and blend
          and it's sex and the *Tao Te Ching* and line-breaks, Anarchism
            lovers & form in poems,
                        & I tell you
        each line in a triolet is a fuse & the scanning
                eye draws fire to the charge of the rhyme
& blows, & sometimes
                    I believe caged birds sing sweetest &

    sometimes wonder why they're caged ——

& you say

The brain is a caged bird —— a parrot ——
The body trapped in its chassis of bone;
But whenever they recite, or race
In a field without fences, they make their own
Small form of freedom, & mould
The too-free sky to a garret
And shape the lowering, cage-cold
Atmosphere to a human space.

3

The body is the great poem

—— Wallace Stevens

Eating the Worm

Adding up the unfinished, the half-full:

This litre of mescal a friend stowed back for you from Mexico in his
       pickup last Christmas,
This ashtray landscaped with dunes and butts from a second friend
      asleep beside you on the floor,
This gathering for a third friend dead a week now, this wake, this
Grief, you guess it should be, somewhere, something keeps you
      rifling inside for a door that opens inward,
This grief mortared up like a corpse in a concrete wall or the sac that
      sealed round the poison in your father's groin after his
      appendix mined him from the inside and the surgeons only
      found it a year later when they cut him open for something else,
This grief you want to drink your way down to, a swimmer in the
      body's slow locks, or afloat in the bottle decending as the
      level crawls toward the worm,

This grief you know now only as numbness, nonbelief
This grief that like the sac in your father's groin is a pocket of poison
      you've got to uproot, slit open and drain or it explodes,
This grief you would like to explode,
This salt like ashes, sand sprinkled on the arroyo formed of your
      thumb and finger you've got to lick clean before sucking back
This bitterness, as if when you fill yourself with liquor with salt you'll
      feel it flood from your eyes all brine and carry off not only
      this guilt but the coffin of your friend, empty, light as a
      shoebox, afloat on the slow locks of the seaway   seaward
This friend who died alone in his house while junk-mail and the
      mail of old friends clattered in through the slot to spread around
      him like a spray of white, fumbled roses, friends passing a few
      feet off in the street friends pausing to finger and smell
      his new-flowering trees, as you did the day he died   as you
      smell and finger now
This worm you've finally reached, poured free, pickled and still, the
      worm you have to eat in some cantina off the road in the
      scavenged Baja in your ribs, your bones, to prove to the patrons
      Yeah you're a man, in your cold white country you can still
      feel, still cry the way a man cries or could for the one beloved
      friend that each friend is, his body
This whole body racked, in time, as if a mirage out of the desert wind
      is shaking, beating me till I hear it cry out *Why? When I was*
      alive, you didn't —— why didn't you love me more, then?

                                        Why?

Dreamer's Boat

(after an etching by Don Maynard)

A saint sailed west out of Ireland
In a coffin of pine, with oars
That cracked the cold waves into foam

And his cape for a sail, and hand
For bailing when the "holy shores"
Fell aft and storm snuffed out the day;

Then devils in a deep wilderness
Of water clung to the bows
& bent over him, whispering *home*

Till his skull filled up with harbours
and hills tolled the summer sun's soft knell
in the childhood of his home

And he asked what drew him away
  to the west, with only stars
for steering and faith as a keel

  To the frozen lee, cliff-shadows
and high fjords of Greenland. Yet out here
        the stars were still in Eden, the Bear

& Scorpion harmless, unnamed;
              constellations blazed like flowers
    in a dark garden, and Jerusalem

towered in the moonlit glacier.
But the voices hissed in his ear

It is not too late —— Bethlehem
lies east, like Ireland, and the fire
in your hearth glows warm.   Go back.
Bite into the fruit of solitude
once, and it grows bitter and hard
to go home.   Go home.
these powers

of the cold air could be patient,
he knew now, as he dragged his boat

onto land   so he stopped listening
and with the bleached pelvis of a goat

for spade, dug down through the frozen
earth till a hole stood ready

for the groundpost and foundation
of a church.
he turned from the chosen
ground to rest   & stretched out by the sea

& dreamed of sailing the longboat

of his ribcage to the next land west

&felt in his bones the cleansing

wind, &   listened to the rains

that churn the surf of that further coast

(& sailed:

"I cannot sleep on the banks of the sea"

Horses of the Sea

Loving you saddle the long wave, galloping,
    grip at the bridle of foam, and the swell
      of ecstasy in an island rising, you

plunge inward with the body's brine
    on tightened thighs and tongue, and slow in the troughs and
      mounting the waves to the crest again and

    I am the wave and the breaker, ride me
over the bay's dark body to the island's
    nearing roar, let your heels dig in to spur and guide me

    as surf rears up snorting and you cling
and breast the grappled spray, hair splashing as
    ripples in the belly mount to a sucking

    riptide you cry over wind and the white, crashing
wave lathered with foam slows the moment up and Ah
    breaks and shatters the body   the rider   the wave

onto pale sand   pulsing   still.
                    Climb down, once more
    human, blind in the breakers, stretch out beside me
    and touch.   As tides slip back and the fluid

moonlight cools, ribs rising   falling in currents
    of sleep, I think of galloping Caspian
      sands —— one beast, mane-dark, coupled to the storm ——

    with hoofs of coral and pearls for eyes.

Highway by the Ocean, Nullarbor Plain

—— *where the desert tumbles like a tranced man*
over sea-cliffs, where a compass, drunk
       with open space, flails
its minute-hand in full evolutions
with no time left to cause

       how a woman   man
might wait hours for their shadow to crawl
like a serpent from the heel's eclipse
       and then elongate, so at evening
the body becomes a timepiece, old
the way a tor on the Serengeti
       is a sundial, a hillside
       is an hourglass
and a peak becomes a timekeeper's candle
burnt away by the elements

       where it gets harder, as the day goes on, going back
to the rusting car,
                    the faint, far breathing of cars on the highway
drowns in a rut between waves, the waves
       of mind and light slacken,
       merge in their idling
                    submerge

(how if you hold
your hand against this sun, your bones
                    will break the dry skin, burst
            free and dance, a shaman
                            over stones,

                                    the clatter
                    as a white reef grins

from shallows where a breaker explodes

            in sun, the chanting of surf —

                                    where the soul

like a handful of salt, dissolves

                    clouds

                            on the wide water

Portrait of a Mother

Red wine spilled in the snow
> so foreign here, you were, your bones not
> marrowed with frost, your
> veins not narrowed brooks
> iced at the shore

A bonfire built on the ice by the ice-fishermen
> hours out on the river, minded till dawn
> by a figure hunched deathbed-
> low, with rod and hatchet, by an eye filming closed

The cinder-dim light of a season's last firefly
> subsiding in the fallow with the field and the skyline
> zippering into flame

Metaxa spilled in the garden
> as dew on the ground-
> pears and peppers a gold, a copper cascading like
> sparks off the grindstone of the sun

The lost incisor
> turning to silver under my ear in the dark hours
> before the bell and the bullies

Thermometer's thin decanter
> refilling itself in the window with red
> wine, a miracle, as winter
> died and the earth warmed and widened

A warmth in air hovering like the breath of herds
> in a manger of the mountains
> in a manger of the sea

Bloodlight pulsing on the escarpment
> to warn the pilot, drunk
> with logic, made blind
> by gauges, GO UP
>   COME DOWN

To the almonds wine and olives, strewn on a table
four legs in the earth —— to red wine

spilled in the snow ——

        (so foreign here, you were, your bones
          not marrowed with frost
              your veins not winter-
     hard streams that I crossed,
        birth-bound,
                  to where you gave me

                     the olive in the stone)

A Thief, Years After

Hide him somewhere & track him down ——
fall marsh smelling of bark-rot, hickory, diesel
under a gap-toothed boardwalk of the Rideau Trail
& the towers of Collin's Bay Pen
cyclopean —— far-off it seems ——
but foreseeable.
                    Dusk
& the army dogs are his shepherds
& lead him into culverts, sewers
with rifle-shot barking they pincer in
                                        (he

like unicorn in thicket gored
while the chateau towers
of Collin's Bay candled & soared
in a Book of long Hours)

                        Spring him April five years down a sentence
nearing its break, & find him
a cave in the clay wall of a reservoir, dry
& each dawn
he rolls clear the esker at the mouth
like a skeptic, rising, unsure of the sun ——
                                        (he

as Christ in gospel helpless, bullets
searing
clear through palms & feet, as double-
crossed, he
falls

        & they send him up again)

                    Send him out, paroled & papered
as a wall
in a rooming house, peel bare
the pale skin of the inside —— outside
in the freshmanned college sunlight September's
pubcrawl chatter of wind in leaves
                                        (& he

in the dropped-out gloaming of almost
dawn, in a line-up of eyes
at the Donut Stop, windowed,
                            Christ no
Christ no unicorn   no hero   no reason
I refuse you —— turn, throw away the poem's
fine, fitting
key

        refuse you)

Near Ephesus

The chimney's always last to go ——
the chimney and the hearth. In woodlots
behind Belfountain, or on this cape
where winds out of Thrace sweep olives
to an early harvest, ruined hovels
will pass unseen —— until the thrust
of chimney above a chilly hearth
undertakes the eye, as a headstone
with its gravity, draws you
down to a common failing.

                         That other hearth
when I found it in early spring
was still stoked with dirty snow;
the walls were gone, and soot-black
cobbles clattered to the forest floor
when I touched the chimney.

                         Yet it made a place for me
to sit —— a warm spot, sunlit, out of the wind ——
and to eat a cold lunch that fuelled
the furnace of my belly, and I almost felt
how it might have been, roofed and fired, the walls festooned
with Christmas decorations ——

No roads left in that woodlot.
A long time, I thought, since anyone else
stopped here to rest. A century at least
since the chimney breathed, or any children
gathered for the sake of gathering.

                         Still
I like to think some notions smoulder
like coals in a cooling grate, long after families

or the lone settler have retired
to rest, after the meal disappears
and gathered friends disperse and the doused mind
cools in sleep —— when winds out of Thrace
are clawing at the olives, cliffs, and below the cape
carcass and fossil flicker with sun ——

the sea sweeping over how many times
without extinguishing that light.

A. D.

Out of the jazz-
Saxophone backstreets, elbowing these
Crowds of the summer night carnival
In alleys

Squirming free of measure like a spiring riff
Or rolled, sweet dazing smoke, gyring into the haze
And high silences
Our Lady of the Snows, where votive

Candles light the eyes of widows, the organ
Stammers in past tenses
And Mary in her frame of icicles, her canticled
        Cave of friezes and stained glass, is half-daughter

To Old Man Order
Apollo.   Twenty centuries of
  alms and slaughter
    rocked in her arms, and I wonder now

  how Jesus of the Jazz
Festival still gliding past each
                chalk-crossed billboard, born
      again in the moment
                        of each first cry (*each
                breath your first   again*)
                                    gets frozen into
  brass & plaster &

                    how the offering of
                love that one night prised wide
             your pores your arms your lips & legs &
                              soul, will close up into codes:
   commandments: the sepalled tree in the ear
                                        of the poet/child
petrified.
             Feel here
        on the line between the steepled
            stasis of icons & the flowering
crowd   why Christ must always shard the glass & limbo
                   free of every icon
                         though he tires in time of the boulevard
                with its masks & markets, & must
                   brace himself in the doorway between them
              not pale in morgue-robes & tamely rapping   but
                         naked and burly   shoulder
                 slammed to the hinge   hammering
             ash to ashes
                             to let air in let incense out
                 evil
                         is not inside the doors or out   evil
                              is whatever dams
                                        the flow
with locks
& walls

        of the woman who loves only what she can cage
        of the man who loves only what he can kill

          Out of the jazz-
saxophone backstreets & into the shrill
high silences of worship, but he is
nowhere to be found, save in the threshold
          between heat & cold, or
          motion & stillness, no
          destination but a door-
          way breathing with wind, my

                    shepherd, the wind
                              is my shepherd

          & the war
                    on the heart

                              is as good as lost

                    like a scholar in the streets of eden

CODAS

Je te verrai bientôt. Je sens que
je te verrai bientôt.

—— Marie-Claire Blais, *La Belle Bête*

In the Light, Wherever Eyes

Leave me. I love her most when her eyes leave me
Sunrise, the sun a pallette of reds she raises
Among olive trees by a dry rill, where she kneels

Painting a scene I'll have to guess —— of the sun
Above a stand of jack pines, by a stream
Brawling with snowmelt, spring —— ?

I see her some ways off   I like the way
   She's become a stone for stillness, seeming to know
How an artist has to disappear

Into landscape and lover
to see them, & scratch the page
            as twigs a frozen tarn, but

   here it's high summer, & hot —— so the leaves
            of this orchard in the foothills
Of the Alpilles, where her pallette is setting

      the mustard afire, grow clenched, and now I see
                  how I love her most when her eyes leave me
         and she is not for me but for the rills
                              the pulsing
            of poppies & sunburned olives & the sea
         for the shadow of her fingers etched into sage
            for a breath,
                        brief drawings

   on the canvas of a field

                        in the light where her eyes lead me

To the Source in Song

Your love as fierce
as the craving of angels, their frozen cries
scored in stars across the night; your love a calling
clear as the ecstasy of the skeptic
in old age, your love a trial
and testament, your love a crux
a crucible, a tundra of thirty years' deep slumber
slapped into life by the lap and gush
of breaking waters, the barrens grassed with sage.
"I must have you at the source," you said, and
"I must have you at the source" and
at the watershed and the snowline under pines and drumlins,
attics in the limestone city and the bars
of West Coast winter nights, will you

fuck me with your body of fire, until the still
sea inside me thaws or fractures
and the brine of my body foams through you
into further seas, into estuaries
upriver still leaping with the Chinook-
salmon for the freshes and the green source, for the salt
walls of the canyons and the water-
fall veiling the rock
face of God. A rill in high ranges wakes with sun
from frozen sleep, and in the still
midnight cirque, flesh quickens around our cries
to a mote floating inside you like the moon

on the calm waters of the mountain pool.

Grace

> *By night on my bed I sought my*
> *beloved. . . . but I found her not.*
>> —— Song of Songs

—— you grew with earth into the years
that crumble, form in cirrus clouds and merge
in tides at the river mouth, and rush
above you like starlings in the wind's gorge
     so now I barely brush against you
without a tang of damp foliage rising, your body
yielding up its musk of turned earth and berries ——

You came down through timber into stone ranges
that farms forgave, found the world
is in love with imperfection
     so now as lips, open to kiss, shape the zero
that circles two round —— twins bellied —— I find no
symmetry no system I could record
     for later repetition.

You see life as a scholar   even poet
never has —— you're the storm they measure, earth
they travel in shoes —— you see
     I confuse you with things I thought other ——

The halogen planets born of roadkilled eyes
The salmon's leap in the flame of a welder
Green sinews of the river, flexing under ice
The métro quaking into underworlds along the iron
     strings of a lyre ——

                      An afternoon I was barely listening
I first heard the cataract upstream, and keepers

frothing at the heart's walls, breezes
in the drumbeat gorges of ears
and though I was not looking
I saw the garden by its smell
from over the barbed wire and floodlit wall:

              Grace

consists in the breaking of skin
and some hour feeling next to dying, stir
to the snowfall drifting through you, turning to rain

in the interior, pooling
into hollows and the grave
sockets of eyes ——

     "As I came down to her
a wind rose off the lake
though I descended it was like climbing a steep trail
my legs trembled as I looked for her
and I was afraid of seeing.
I searched everywhere along the shore but found no sign.
I went to the end of the pier and saw nothing
but islands, white sails, and the far shoreline
shivering.
     Then I heard her speak."

Homer

If time is a Greek island
and we come from the sea
and rest from the climb on a ledge up in the wind-
animate sage and lavender, far inland, looking back

down the ivory highlands to the sea
you see a solid page
poemed with highways, histories, signposts and cities and
in the haze at the chalk margins of the land

loud, illiterate seas grinding the littoral
—— each wave out there an unrecorded year ——
waves spanning off to the eye's own shore
where sight topples, swallowed into the sea, and all vision

sinks away.
            If time is a Greek island
a few thousand years of voices behind us
bubble their scriptures, slogans, grocery lists
—— sounds low and overlapping as the waves that always

always behind me I hear and
drowned in the monoxide roaring of cities but
            still, from the edge of the sea where language
first grounded firm and left its prints, a voice

carries, barely, but
so raw   real   so clear and
primal it lungs up over the years and over
other voices closer in time and

technique, and still
from the lip of a distant cliff, dissolving,
half-drowned by howling breakers, a bare man
clings to the chalk above the shingle, ankles

manacled with seaweed, seawrack, while the foaming
mouth just level with the land, wide-open, sings
above the babel of the sea, so somehow
bridging years arched up from the cave

to the penthouse suite, over winedark
screams that stain the land
as history, we might hear him still
overdue, over everything, might hear him sing ——

                    and we hear him still,

                             sing:

Muse,

  sing me the fury of Peleus' son
Achilles, brutal and doomed, who cost the Acheans
dearly, & cast down

so many souls into the mass grave
of no man's land —— brave
  bodies fodder for the mines &

      machine guns &

so fulfilled
the famished will

of God.
  Muse sing first
of the clash and the sundering

    of Lord Agamemnon

  and Achilles ——

    & cry,
      like a later bard
   of arms
     & the child ——

The Machine Gunner

I saw them. They came like ghosts out of ground-
mist, moving
over ruined earth in waves, running

no, walking, shoulder to shoulder
like a belt of bullets or like
men: tinned meat lined on a conveyor belt as the sun

exploded in thin shafts on metal
buckles, bayonets, the nodding
spires of helmets. I heard faint battle cries

and whistles, piercing through the shriek
of fire and iron falling, the slurred
cadence of big guns. As they funnelled

like a file of mourners into gaps
in the barbed wire I made quick
calculations and slipped the safety catch.

But held my fire. Alongside me
the boys in the trenches worried them with
rifles, pistols, hand grenades

but they came on, larger now, their faces
almost resolving out of hazed hot
distance, their ranks at close quarters amazing

with dumb courage, numb step, a sound of drugged
choking in gas and green mud, steaming ——
Who were these men. I saw them penitent

sagging to knees. I saw their dishevelled
dying. And when finally they broke
into a run it came to me

what they had always been, how I'd always,
really, seen them: boys
rushing toward us with arms

outstretched, hands clenched as if in urgent prayer,
sudden welcome or a reunion
quite unexpected. Yes. And more than this

like children, chased by something behind the lines
and hurrying to us
for rescue ——

I spat and swung the gun around. Fired,
felt the metal pulse
and laid them three deep in the wire.

Nomansland

In your landlord's garden, summer is a lease
you no longer remember signing.
Swallow-calls from behind the hedgerow
blend with the cicada drone
of the dynamo, the crystal wingbeat of the dragonfly
& fall silent. In late August,
evenings, first notice arrives
of the mellow air's eviction.

In that garden, autumn
is an old man's Lent
that makes the spirit lean with fasting.
Swallowed by the insatiable air
geese scale the light in summits of gliding
feathers & bone. Their shadows on the earth
are a fleeting windfall, famine
in a crop of moulding apples. Hours
falling back into darkness.

From a chilly foyer, through windows
white with a fine print of frost
you see winter in your landlord's garden
cloud the soil, as a slow cataract in time
crawls, glacial, over each cinema-
idol's eye. He is an absentee
landlord, who leaves his tenants each winter
with meaningless drafts, & a vacancy
cold, like glass, & bitter
as a bough red with frozen berries.

Spring is promissory, zealous as the land-
lord's garden flowers with noons, promiscuous
tendrils, moisture & seeds, the ovaries of the hummingbird
brimming. This moment
pilfered from the world's spin
seems in your fist like a finished contract, here
in the garden, where the world expires
in perpetuity, & the words begin
to an ovation of weeds & wet blossoms
at the summer air's inception.

Psalm 90

You. Who've been our Eden since we came ——

Hours before the mountains slid
dorsal from the waters, & the land
dried, & children first grew on the shores of the world,
cries echoing
                          you were here: green pebble
plunging through the wind-
tunnels of space, you stirred this life
into being, squeezed blood and the brief
limbs of lovers' edens
from your molten womb.

We're swallowed, after the ecstasy & mourning,
swallowed by stars & swaddled in cold
consoling soil —— not crushed
by the wrath of some random god ——

        This Eden, earth, let your   passing be in us
in the moment in movement, in failed still-
fertile bulbs, these fallen pine needles
pressed into heels,
                          as we drift,
a galaxy of seeds, through barren hills
more beautiful than gardens.

Wedding: Annapurna Sanctuary

       Now with this phrase we bring each other
into the old circle where layers
of couples love and merge like these mingled
       summits that ring us

       And I give this ring in the conviction
there are some traditions that do not chain us
but let us link fingers only reaching back
through the ranges of generation
to sanctuaries where others flattened moss and walked
       under snow-histories like these . . .

       So feel: warm strata under sheets of ice,
sun's heat finding the glacier, in this mountain chain
       we are free —— two seeds
released into life by their meeting ——
       the ring I give, you will easily slip through
       routed to larger, to higher circles, you
       climbing clear through a wellmarked pass
to widen the form of footprints followed
by a mass of others your hand is warmed

Were You to Die

Were you to die I'd be free to go off
and see the world, and sleep in every elsewhere
I might never arrive
—— yet I might choose to travel alone
from window to window looking out
on the streets of your city
where your friends still expect to see you sometimes
or mistake you for someone, out of custom —— love ——

Without your thrashing, manic dreams, my body
would sleep better
but wake more tired, I'd let the garden go to seed
the way I always meant to
and when I looked out the window into the yard
I'd never miss the snowpeas, beets and roses
but your sunhat I might miss —— you hunkered down
in a summer dress, your fingers
grouped like roots in the raised beds,
your stooped, stubborn nape, your cinnamon-
freckled shoulders ——

Were you to die, my heart
would be free to pack a bag
and book passage for the riot of islands
I might have been, and shared
with the one and numberless "beloved" we fumble
our whole lives glimpsing
a moment too late
when Eden was always the one who stayed
rooted in her changes, and gave you
the island in her arms, and when you slept
somehow she travelled, and when you woke
she was changed ——

Were you to die, my mind
would be free to twist inward
the way fingers fist, and fasten pat
on its own taut notions, theorems, palm shut fast
to the snow that pooled there and seemed to flow through
when the skin still flowered in fullest winter
and I loved you, and thoughts, like books,
were doors that opened outward
not coffins, closed,
not cells ——

Were you to die and free me
my body would follow you down into the cold
prison of your passing, and warm you when all the others
had turned away, and try
bribing the keeper with a poem, or fool him
with keychains of chiming words —— an elegy .
so pure he'd be pressed to cry, eyes
thawing and the earth warmed, April
of carillons and sepals, your opened arms
that bore the sun down with you, warm.

Tonight in the winter pine-tops
under a moon, this roaring —

is it the wind in the branches
or the slow burn of stars?

Elegy For E.M.J.

(Brockville, 1896-1990)

Pulled down in a riptide of rushing years
she fought for breath as her body, time-logged, sank
into waters shoaled with ageing births:
$$\text{the rippling}$$
hands of the midwife, salt-streamed eyes
of a new daughter   son
stripped now of names and flesh and calling

calling out to her as the waters break
and run into the salt salmon delta
and ferry her on, out of sound.

                    At the end
in the "home," bottled in sick-
bays of foundering daylight, trapped with a skeleton
crew of chattering   dissolving   *I do*
recall you from somewhere I do   she must have
prayed for a brief last breath
to belly her sails and take her back . . .

                    She's gone
but not far enough, I guess. In fields
swelling green as a   *green as a*
—— lifeboat is lowered off decks of grass
while we, the thinning crew, look on, our own descent
impending.
          Feeling

this riptide of rushing years, like the heave
when we left your body. Out past these white-capped
breakers of stone, the infant cries
of Danish freighters bound
downriver for the sea.
                    Then rocky soil like a tide
casting up a wreck's rudder (now free like the dead
not to steer but be borne) courses in
and we turn away, for   home: new again
she's launched and baptized by the cold
continuous roaring of fossil waves.

The Ecstasy of Skeptics

EXIT signs in the scholars' hallway
Lead through polished sheets of plate glass
Into air into thin air —

                              outborne
From an ivory silence
Where the world was to be rephrased
Where the skeleton key of learned
Rigour, cracks
Feckless in the lock, where screens
Glow green as chlorophyll (or
Landfill, breeding —a Babel
Of cavilled, rootless words that mean,
In the heart's hearing, what?)

                              This tongue
is a moment of moistened dust, it must learn
to turn the grit of old books
into hydrogen, and burn
The dust of the muscles must burn
down the blood-fuse of the sinews, the tendons'
taut wick, these bones like tinder giving light
to read by, and heat, the winter light is already
lagging, we'll soon be less than cinders, adrift
in an aftermath of space . . .

Voices in the scholars' hallway
lead through fastened doors
into catacombs of jargon, parchment hives.

Now, love. This way. With the lights on. Blazing.

Acknowledgements

A number of people made comments —— often unrepeatable ——
about some of the poems in this book, and I'm grateful for their
honesty. My thanks to Brian Bartlett, Don Coles, George Elliott
Clarke, Maggie Helwig, Michael Holmes, Janet Madsen, Peter
Ormshaw, Al Purdy, Jay Ruzesky, Mark Sinnett, Anne Szumigal-
ski, Chris Wiseman, and the editors of the magazines listed
below. A few other people were singled out for harsher treatment
and wound up reading the whole thing; I'm especially thankful
to Mary Cameron, Carl Grindley, John and Lambie Heighton,
and C.P.A. expert Don McKay, who readied the book for the
press. Thanks as well to Michael B. Davis, Martha Sharpe, and
Kaari Turk at House of Anansi Press.

Mary Huggard was, as always, my first reader. And my fiercest.

And for his guidance the whole way through, my very special
thanks to Michael Redhill.

Earlier versions of some of these poems first appeared in:
*Arc, Brick, Canadian Literature, Carousel, Crash, The Dalhousie Re-
view, Dandelion, Descant, Estuaire, Event, Exile, The Fiddlehead, Kan-
sas Quarterly* (USA), *Lines Review* (UK), *The Literary Review* (USA),
*The Moosehead Review, New Canadian Review, The New Quarterly,
Oversion, Poem* (USA), *Poetry Canada, PRISM international, Proser-
pine Press, Quadrant* (Australia), *Revue Europe* (France), *The Under-
ground Review, Vintage '91* (Sono Nis, 1992), *Written in Stone*
(Quarry Press, 1993), *Zymergy*.

Earlier versions of "Dylan's Source" and "The Machine Gun-
ner" appeared in *Stalin's Carnival* (Quarry Press, 1989). Thanks to
the press for permission to use them.

The third section of "Takayama" is after a poem by a Japanese
poet of the Heian period, Ono Komachi.

The assistance of the Ontario Arts Council and the Banff Centre
for the Arts is gratefully acknowledged.

"Psalm: Hands of the Beautiful Swimmers" is for Janet, Peter,
and Mary. "A Triolet, Abandoned" is for Jay.